APR 2 7 2005

DATE DUE

MY BODY

My Nose

By Lloyd G. Douglas

Welcome Books™

Children's Press®
A Division of Scholastic Inc.
New York / Toronto / London / Auckland / Sydney
Mexico City / New Delhi / Hong Kong
Danbury, Connecticut

Photo Credits: Cover © Ariel Skelley/Corbis; p. 5 © Laura Dwight/Corbis; pp. 7, 21 (top left) © Lauren Shea/Photo Researchers; pp. 9, 21 (top right) © Eyewire; pp. 11, 21 (bottom left) © C/B Productions/Corbis; p.13 © Derek Berwin/Getty Images; p.15 © Gabrielle Revere/Getty Images; p.17 © Britt Erlanson/Getty Images; pp. 19, 21 (bottom right) © Sean Justice/Getty Images.
Contributing Editor: Shira Laskin
Book Design: Michael de Guzman

Library of Congress Cataloging-in-Publication Data

Douglas, Lloyd G.
    My nose / by Lloyd G. Douglas.
    p. cm. — (My body)
    Summary: A simple introduction to the anatomy and functions of the
nose, discussing the nostrils, smelling, and sneezing.
    ISBN 0-516-24063-3 (lib. bdg.)—ISBN 0-516-22132-9 (pbk.)
    1. Nose—Juvenile literature. 2. Smell—Juvenile literature. [1.
Nose. 2. Smell. 3. Senses and sensation.] I. Title. II. Series.

QP458.D68 2003
612.8'6—dc22

                                                          2003014454

Contents

I have a nose.

5

My nose has two holes called **nostrils**.

7

Our noses help us **breathe**.

Air goes into our noses through our nostrils.

We also use our noses to smell.

There are many kinds of smells.

Smoke and other bad smells let us know that the air is not safe.

13

Sometimes, dust and dirt get inside our noses.

We **sneeze** when this happens.

15

After we sneeze, we use **tissues** to wipe our noses.

17

People often hold their noses while they **swim**.

They do not want water to get inside their nostrils.

19

Noses are very **useful** parts of our bodies.

21

New Words

breathe (**breeth**) to take air in and out of your body
through your nose or your mouth

nostrils (**noss**-truhlz) the two openings in your nose
through which you breathe and smell

smoke (**smohk**) the gray or black cloud of gas that
rises in the air when something burns

sneeze (**sneez**) to push air out through your nose
and mouth suddenly, often because you have
a cold

swim (**swim**) to move through water using the arms
and legs or the fins, flipper, or tail

tissues (**tish**-ooz) soft, thin papers used for wiping

useful (**yoos**-fuhl) helpful

To Find Out More

Books
Knowing about Noses
by Allan Fowler
Grolier Publishing

The Holes in Your Nose
by Genichiro Yagyu
Amanda Mayer Stinchecum, translator
Kane/Miller Book Publishers

Web Site
The Nose Knows
http://www.kidshealth.org/kid/body
Learn the different parts of the nose and how they work.

Index

About the Author
Lloyd G. Douglas has written many books for children.

Reading Consultants
Kris Flynn, Coordinator, Small School District Literacy, The San Diego County
    Office of Education

Shelly Forys, Certified Reading Recovery Specialist, W.J. Zahnow Elementary
    School, Waterloo, IL

Paulette Mansell, Certified Reading Recovery Specialist, and Early Literacy
    Consultant, TX